PAPER QUILLING FOR BEGINNERS

A Step By Step Guide With Pictures And Illustrations To Learn And Master The Techniques To Do Paper Quilling And Projects

Copyright@2020

Deli Hop

1

Table Of Content

CHAPTER ONE

Introduction To Paper Quilling

Paper quilling or paper filigree is an art form that entails the utilization of strips of paper that are rolled, formed or shaped, and glued together to make ornamental designs. The paper is rolled, looped, curled, twisted and otherwise control to produce shapes which make up designs to beautify greetings cards, boxes, pictures, eggs, and to make models, mobiles, jewelry etc. Paper quilling begins with rolling a strip of paper into a coil and afterward pinching the coil into shapes that can be joined or glued together. There are advanced methods and varied sized paper that are utilized to make 3D miniatures, flowers, abstract art, and portraits amid several things.

What do I need to start quilling?

You don't actually need a lot to begin quilling. You just need a number of quilling strips and a quilling tool.

Quilling strips are simply thin pieces of paper that are curled into shapes by utilizing a quilling tool, and afterward joined to make raised patterns and amazing designs on your cards and papercraft projects.

Paper types

Quilling paper is accessible on the consumer market in more than 250 colors and dimensions. It can be divided down into a variety of groups, such as solid colored, two-tone, graduated, acid-free, and other mixed parcels of quilling paper. It is available in different dimensions, like 1/8", ¼" and 3/8" or 3mm, 5mm, 7mm and 10mm paper parcels. However, 5mm is the most commonly utilized size.

Acid-Free

As the name obviously specifies, this is a paper that is entirely acid free. The quality makes it an excellent choice for making rubber stamping, scrapbooks, and creating frames for pictures. It guarantees your project will last a lifetime, devoid of any side effects on the album or framed picture.

Graduated

This kind of paper provides an outstanding look to ornamental quilling projects. The edges encompass a solid color that slowly fades to white. When utilizing a graduated paper, a quilling ring starts with a dark shade but ends up being faded to a lighter side. On the contrary, a number of graduated papers start as white, or a lighter shade, and then gradually fades into a solid, darker color.

Two-Tone

This is another significant kind of quilling paper. It is pretty similar to the graduated quilling paper in its utilization. The look comprises a concrete color on one side and relatively lighter color on the other side. With two-tone paper the color stays or remains same, however the concentration of color differs. The major utilization of this quilling paper is to make available a preferred level of smoothness or softness to the quilled subject. It has the ability to quill several papers in a single spiral.

CHAPTER TWO

Paper Quilling Tools And Materials

The tools below are useful for paper quilling:

Slotted Quilling Tool

This tool enables you to place a quilling strip into the slot. All you have to do is to roll the tool and make a coil without the paper sliding around. The slot does leave a slight crimp in the middle of each spiral, which might not be to your liking.

In all, a slotted tool is utilized for rolling the strips of quilling paper into a coil. A toothpick can as well be utilized to roll the paper strip however the coil will display a bigger hole in the middle.

Needle Tool

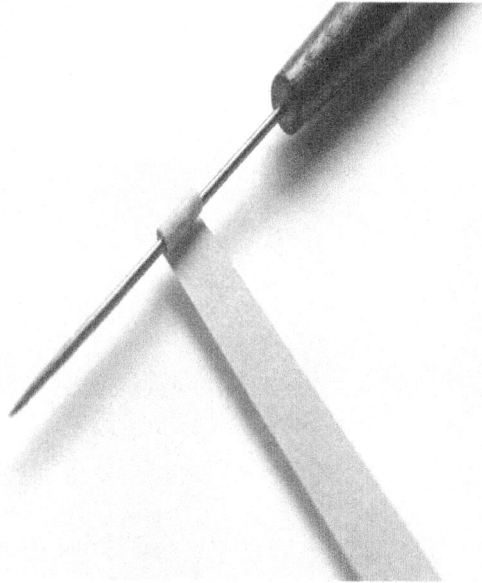

With the help of the needle tool, you can curl the paper around the point and into a tiny, perfect coil — without a crimp. It requires a little practice to get the hang of it, and to make coils swiftly.

Paper Bead Tools

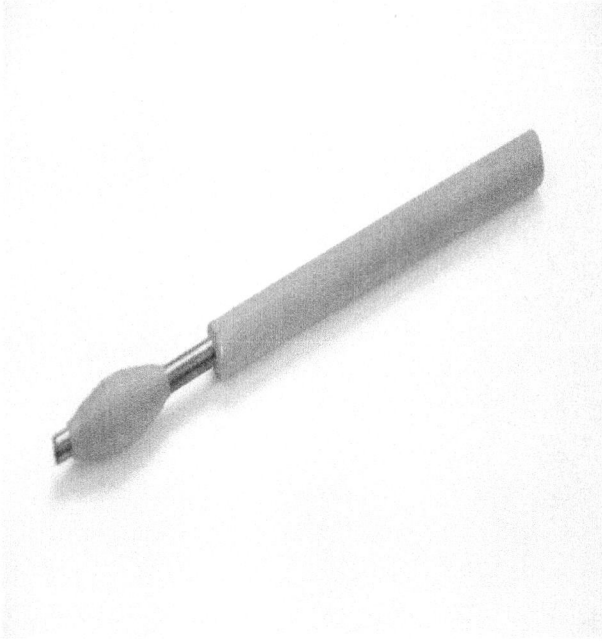

These look and work similar to the slotted quilling tool, but can accommodate broader cuts and many strips of paper at once. And they are quite fast!

Scissors

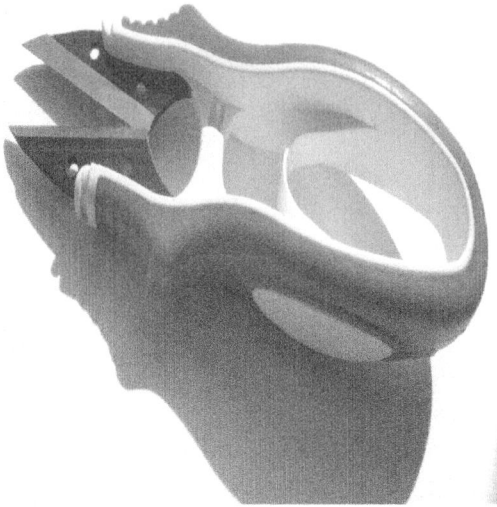

You need scissors if you are working with paper.
Thread snipper is a must for sewing projects, make
superb tiny cuts.

Quilling Paper

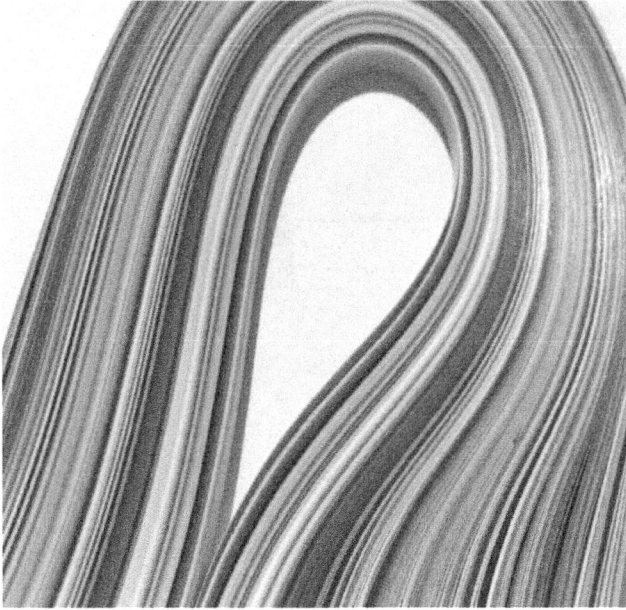

Of course, there is no way you can quill without paper. However, it is quite unfortunate that many crafters don't give adequate attention to the quality of paper being used. The quality of paper being used will also determine the beauty of your project. Hence, there is need to look for specifically designed quilling paper in a range of colors, weights, widths and finishes.

Crimpers

If you're quilling with kids, you will need a quilling crimper to make zigzag shapes you can tenderly roll into loose coils.

Quilling Forms

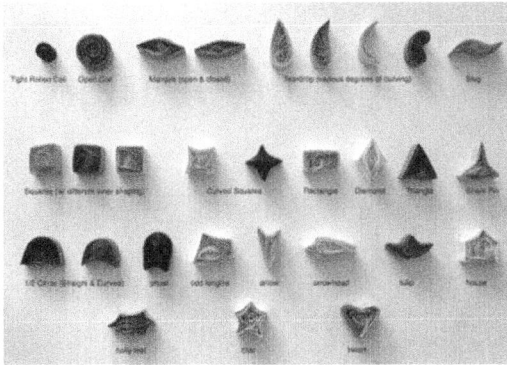

Quilling forms enable you to design and roll additional free-form projects.

Needle Forms

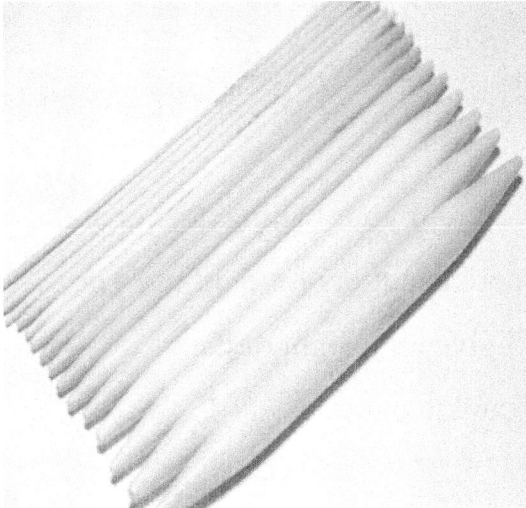

It allows quillers to create many sizes of small rings including very tiny ones.

Cookie Cutters

Of course, you can raid your baking drawer and make utilize of cookie cutters for quilling. The photo above will give an insight of the usefulness of cookie cutter.

Quilling Molds

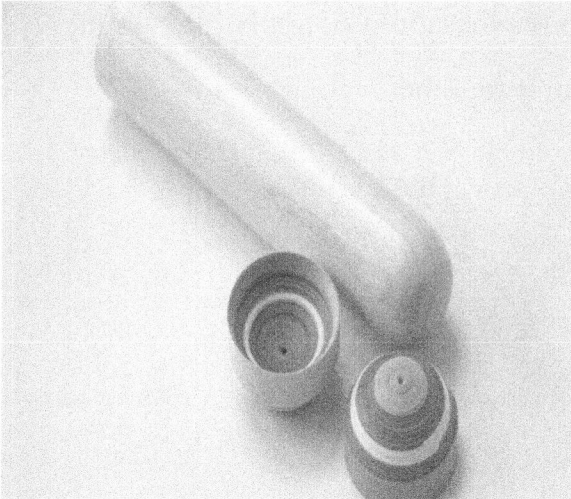

You need quilling molds if you're into 3D quilling. You tenderly place a tight coil over the fittingly sized mold and glide the paper downward to formulate a dome. Once you take it off the mold you can keep on shaping it or apply glue on the inside to cling it together.

Placing two paper domes together can make beads or spheres or other incredible designs.

You will as well need fringing scissors for making paper flowers. Of course, you can utilize regular scissors, but the five blades in these special scissors create little strips that work absolutely for ornamental blossoms.

Quilling Comb

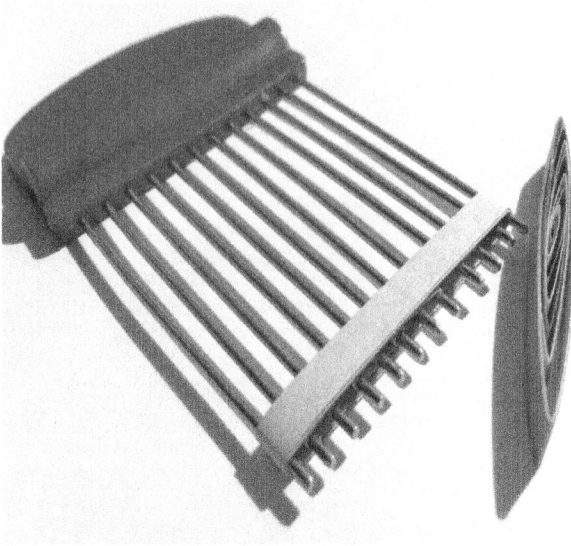

If flowers and landscapes give you quilling bliss, you will definitely need a quilling comb. This tool makes intricately laced loops that you can weave into a various patterns.

Quilling Guides

Quilling guides can be of an immense help for newbie quillers or kids who desire try this paper craft. Just slide your slotted quilling tool in the guide before inserting the paper, and you are all set to roll. The flat surface enables help coils to stay put without springing open suddenly.

Quilling Board

Whenever you need to make a lot of coils of the same size, the paper quilling template board is a perfect tool to have. The circle templates on the quilling board will help you to hold each coil to the accurate size and measurement.

Tweezers

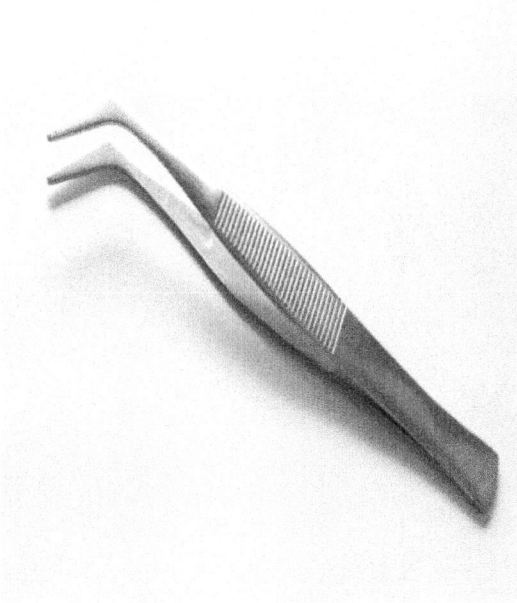

Angled tweezers is needed to glue or place small pieces into your coils.

Circle Sizers

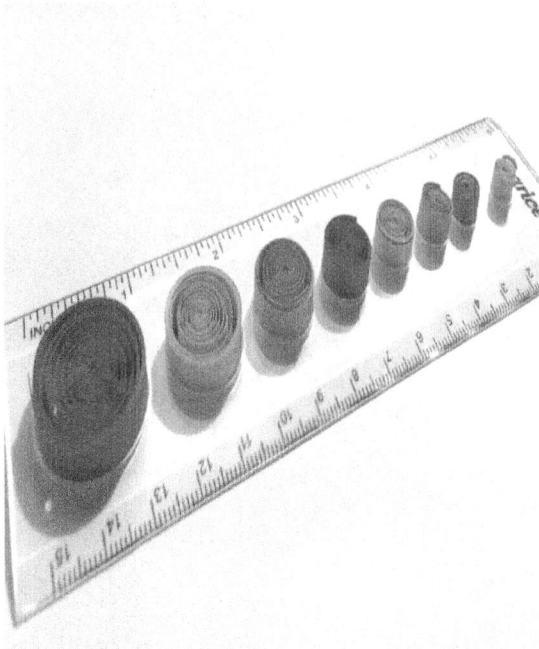

Just starting to quill? As a newbie, it is better to get a circle sizer. Its recessed spaces can enable you make the constantly sized shapes you require. Some come with a ruler, others have extra openings.

Quilling Glue

Any craft glue can to utilize on the loose ends of the paper strips. Utilize the glue sparingly on the quilling paper. A toothpick can be utilized for applying the glue.

The choice of glue you use depends on you, however, get the one that is simple to use with a needle-nosed bottle as well.

Paper Fringer

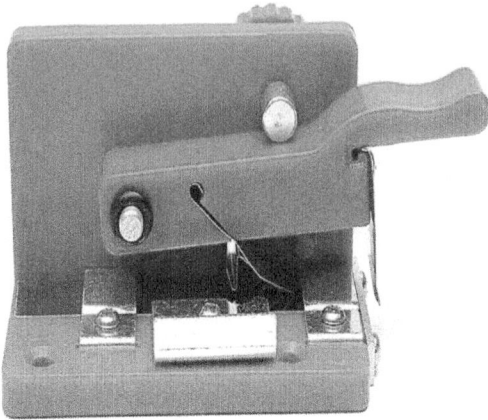

The paper fringer is being used for making fringes on a strip of quilling paper quickly. Fringing can also be done using a pair of scissors but it takes longer time to do it and the paper at times does not turn out completely fringed. The fringed quilling paper is utilized to make fringed flowers.

Bulldog Clip

When making fringing manually with a pair of scissors, a bulldog clip is utilized as a guide during cutting when making fringing manually with a pair of scissors. It can further be utilized to hold numerous strips for quilling paper together for fringing with a pair of scissors.

CHAPTER THREE

Paper Quilling Tips for Beginners

8 Tips To Help You Become A Quilling Pro

Paper quilling, also known as paper filigree, is a papercraft that has been popular since the 15th century. This paper art has encountered resurgence in popularity during the last couple of years.

You can find paper quilling integrated into scrapbooking, monograms, cardmaking, paper flowers, jewelry and even into pieces of wall art. It is amazing how you can make complicated shapes and patterns from simple paper strips and glue! Even though the hobby is quite easy to master, beginners may discover the following tips and tricks helpful on their paper quilling journey.

Make use of Pre-cut Paper Strips for Your First Projects

Utilize pre-cut paper quilling strips for your first projects. Your initial attempts will have better results if you make use of accurate machine-cut papers. Once you are at ease with basic paper quilling techniques, you can cut your paper strips and travel around your creativity by experimenting with additional advanced methods.

Start With Small Paper Quilling Projects

Begin with smaller sized projects first. You can swiftly become overwhelmed when trying to tackle a craft project that is too complex or too large.

Small projects can encourage feelings of success and accomplishment and can be the building blocks the help you master your skills one step at a time. After you have mastered the basics, you can attempt complex projects with ease.

Utilize the Right Paper Quilling Tools

It is significant to choose your quilling tools considerately. You don't have to to purchase any

expensive tools to create paper filigree art initially–
a toothpick or bamboo skewer will roll paper strips
effectively. If you are bitten by the paper quilling
bug and desire to continue, you should purchase a
slotted quilling tool and a needle tool.

You can put the strip of paper into the upper slot of
the slotted tool, giving you additional control when
rolling the paper strips. A needle tool is a sizeable
tapered needle with a long wooden handle. It helps
you maintain a steady hand while rolling strips of
paper into diverse shapes. Both tools are pretty
helpful when you are working on large, complex
paper quilling projects.

Have a Light Touch When Utilizing Glue with Paper Quilling

When gluing your rolled paper shapes, at all times remember to utilize glue sparingly. Too much glue can speedily ruin your project, which you might have worked on for hours. You can prevent the hassle of beginning a project afresh by applying a bit of caution. You can at all times add a bit more glue if essential, but cannot take away excess glue. Bear in mind the design rule 'Less is More.'

Paper Quilling Patterns

Some beginners find using a premade quilling pattern pretty helpful when first starting out. There are hundreds of paper quilling patterns available to buy. These patterns can guide beginners and enable them build their skills.

All you need to do is place the printed pattern underneath a sheet of waxed paper and follow the recommendations. You will speedily have a quilling "masterpiece" that you will be proud to offer as a gift or exhibit in your home.

Master the Basic Paper Quilling Shapes

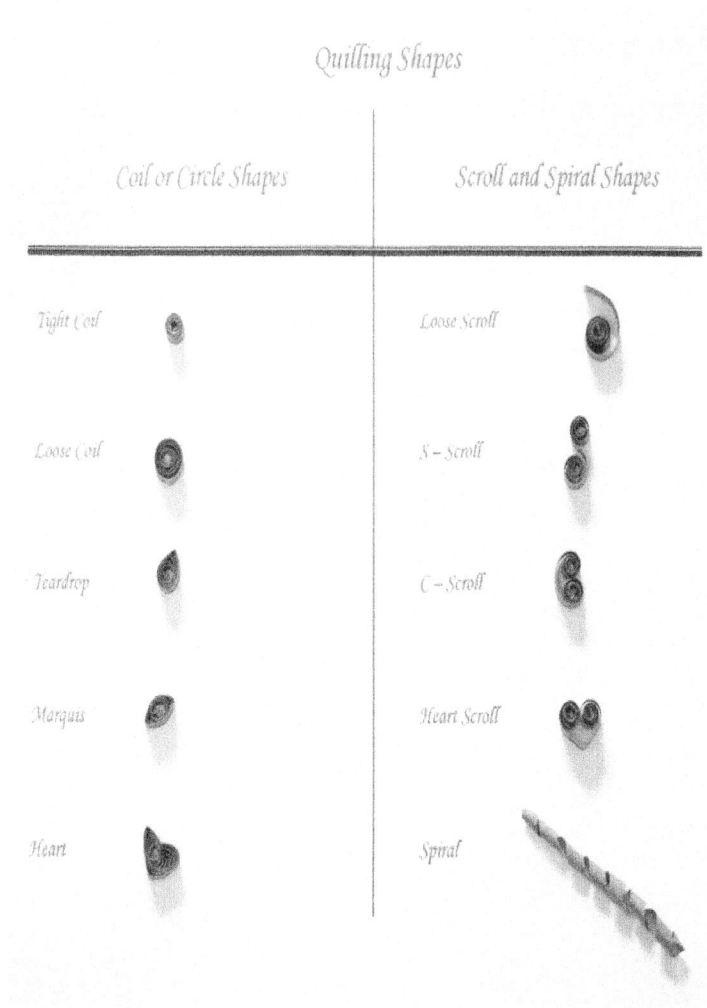

Quilling Shapes

Coil or Circle Shapes	Scroll and Spiral Shapes
Tight Coil	Loose Scroll
Loose Coil	S – Scroll
Teardrop	C – Scroll
Marquis	Heart Scroll
Heart	Spiral

There is need to learn the basic shapes before working on a paper quilling project. It can be pretty helpful to make a master page of basic paper quilling shapes.

Glue various shapes to a piece of cardboard to utilize as a reference sheet when working on different projects. The guide functions as both a reference point and an inspiration source.

Paper Quilling Circle Sizing Board

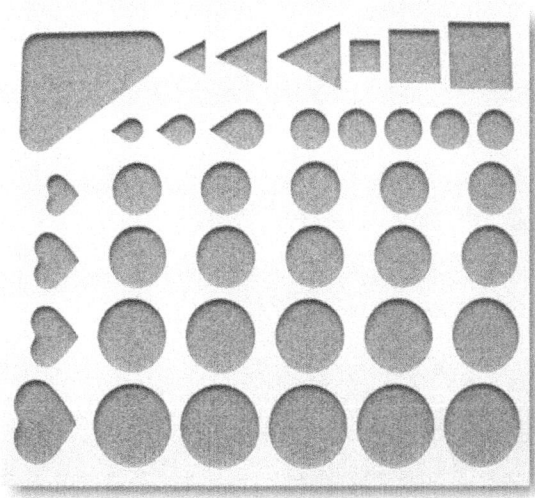

A circle sizing board is a tool you absolutely will find helpful. It is a sheet of plastic that has predrilled holes of different shapes and sizes. Utilize the holes to help you roll the paper quilling shapes.

The circle sizing board will enable you to always have uniformity in your paper quilling shapes. This board is a tool you won't want to be without and will utilize again and again.

Acetate Sheet

You should build your paper quilling rolled shape onto a sheet of acetate. It is strong enough to provide your glued quilled shapes firmness. Once the glue has dried, you can pull your quilled piece up off the sheet with no damage. Simply wash the leftover glue from the acetate sheet and re-use for your subsequent project.

Paper Quilling Closing Thoughts

These are simply a few tips to help you get started on your paper quilling journey. Bear in mind that it will take a little time to master the craft, so be patient with yourself and practice. You will discover that if you keep at it, you will be amazed with your progress. You will shortly be making pieces of quilling art that are gorgeous and will be cherished by you and everyone you offer a paper quilling project as a gift.

CHAPTER FOUR

How To Make Coils With Quilling Paper Strips

You have to get a strip of quilling paper and insert one end into the slit of a slotted quilling tool.

Begin turning the quilling tool and the quilling paper will wrap around the tool to shape a coil.

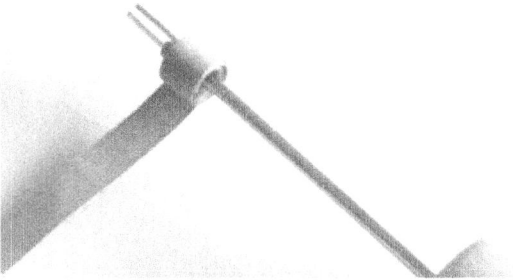

Continue turning the quilling tool until it gets to the other end of the quilling paper. Cautiously remove the coil from the tool and allow it unwind a bit to make a loose coil.

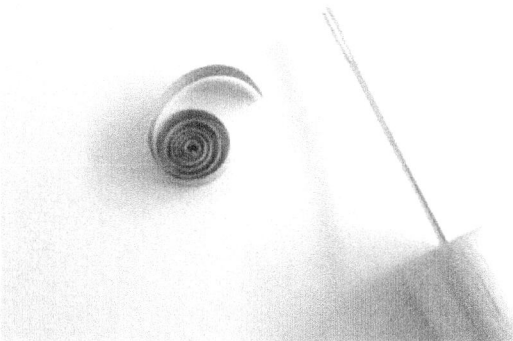

Apply a little glue to the free end of the paper and stick it to the coil.

Utilize quilling papers with a range of colours to create coils of diverse shapes and sizes. The following quilled shapes can be created by means of pressing and pinching the round coils using your fingers.

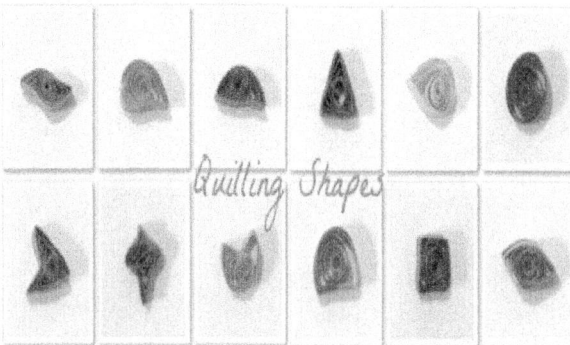

Quilling Shapes

CHAPTER FIVE

How To Make Tight Coils in Paper Quilling Art

To create a tight coil, get one end of a strip of quilling **paper** and insert it into a slotted quilling tool.

Ensure to hold the paper using one hand and the quilling tool using the other hand.

Begin to turn the tool to roll the strip of paper.

Put a little of tension on the paper so that it does not come loose.

Continue to turn the tool until the other end of the quilling paper becomes extremely short.

Using a toothpick, apply a little glue on the paper to stick it to the coil and grasp the shape in place. To create bigger coils, connect numerous strips of quilling paper together to obtain a long strip of paper.

To create multi-coloured tight coils, utilize numerous quilling paper strips of diverse colours joined together.

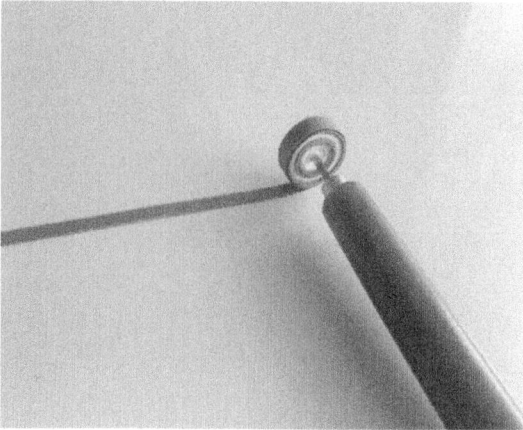

CHAPTER SIX

How To Do Quilling

Thing you will need

- Slotted quilling tool

- Quilling strips

- Glue

- Ruler

- Quilling comb

- Paper scrap making tool (to make strips if you need)

Section 1- Learning The Basics

1 - Identify the two different types of paper curling tools.

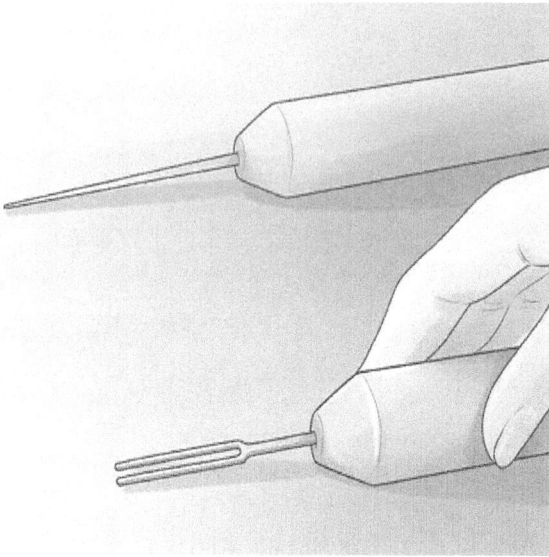

These two2 tools are the needle tool and the slotted tool. The slotted tool is best for learners, while the needle tools fit itself to an increasingly perfect creation. You can also make use of a toothpick or corsage needle if you do not prefer to purchase both of these tools.

- Slotted tool: This is slim pencil-like instrument with a slit or slot at the top. The one downside of the slotted tool is that it makes a tiny crimp in the middle of the paper where you slide the paper into the top of the tool. If this doesn't trouble you then you should definitely attempt this device when you are first beginning.

- Needle tool: This tool is difficult to utilize however will bring about an uncrimped (which means it looks more professional) and ideal spiral.

2 - Make or purchase your quilling strips.

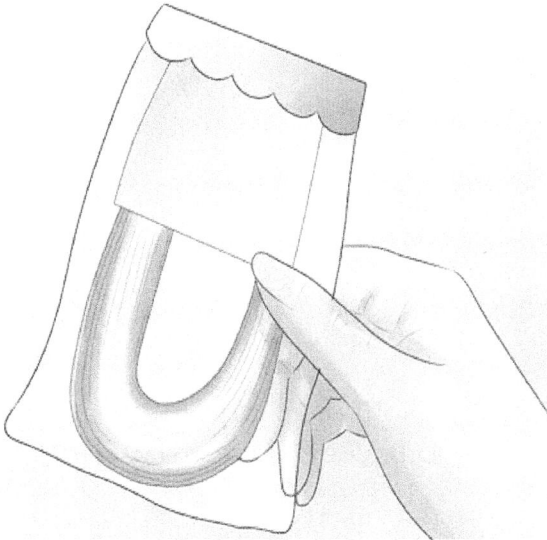

The art of quilling is based, of course, on the paper utilized to make your pieces of art. Quillers make use of thin strips of colorful paper, curling them with their tools to make amazing designs. You can create your own strips by cutting bits of paper into equal-sized strips, or you can purchase pre-cut paper. The length of your strips will rely upon on the pattern that you are following.

3 - Try coiling the paper.

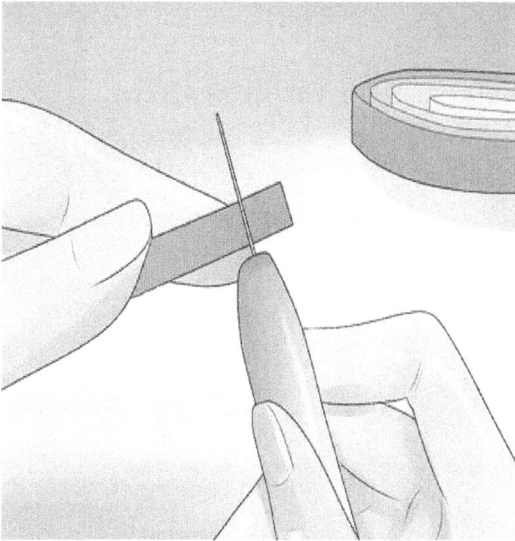

Before you create any cool decor, make a lot of plain coils. To begin, insert one end of a quilling strip into the tiny slot in your quilling instrument.

Ensure it is nice and snug, then begin twirling the tool away from you. The paper ought to wrap around the end of the quilling tool, making a coil. Continue twirling the paper until the entire quilling strip is being twisted on the quilling tool.

- To attempt coiling with a needle tool or toothpick, get your fingers a bit damp and afterward curve one end of paper strip around the needle (or other tool). Utilize your thumb and forefinger to apply weight and roll the paper around the needle.

Section 2 – Gluing Your Designs

1 - Gently pull the coil off.

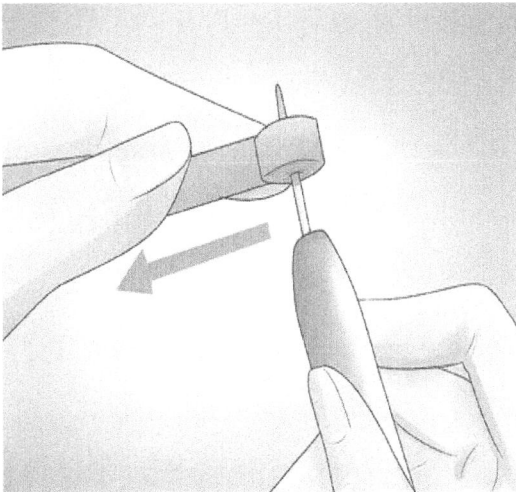

When the piece of paper has been rolled all the way around your tool, take it off. If you need a loose coil, put it down and allow it loosen.

2 - Glue your paper together.

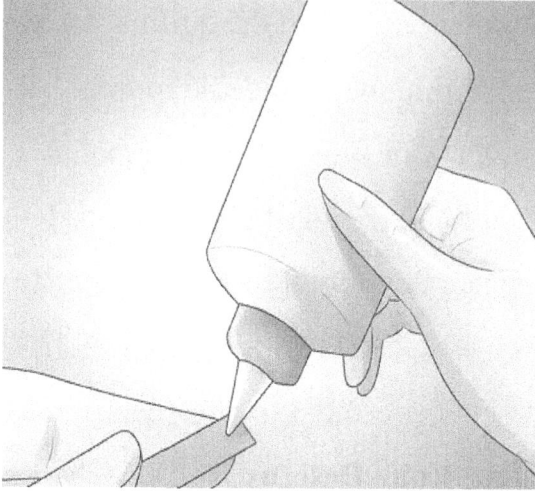

Once the coil is as large or small as you desire it, glue the tail. You ought to only apply a little amount of glue. Utilize a toothpick, paper piercing tool, or T-pin to dab a little quantity of glue on the inside side of the end of the paper (the tail). Make sure to hold for twenty seconds.

- Basic glue, such as Elmers, will work very well for quilling. You can also give tacky glue a try, as it dries more faster than basic glue. You can further attempt water-based super glue, which dries amazingly faster and holds the paper well.

3 - Pinch the coil into a shape if you like.

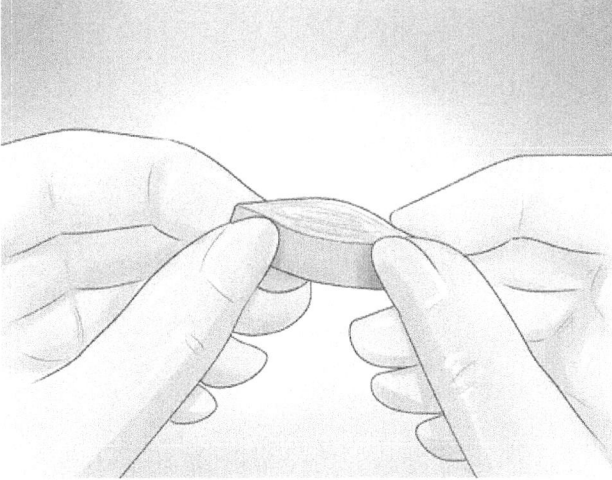

The pattern you are following will determine whether you will do this or not. You might desire to pinch it into an eye shape for a leaf. You can likewise do a triangle for an ear. The possibilities are limitless!

4 - Glue all your pieces together.

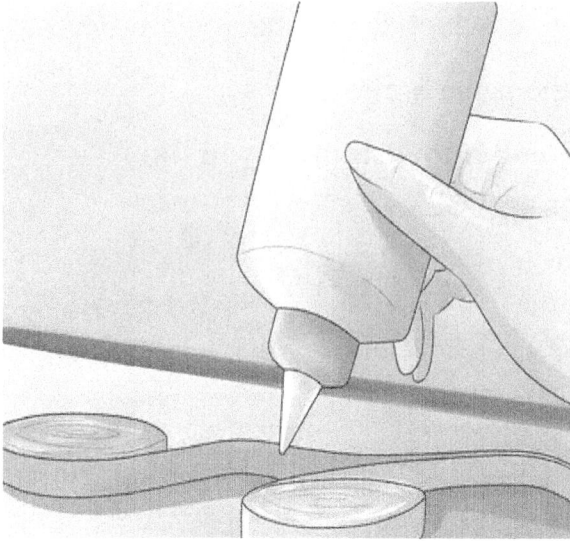

Once more, be very careful and prudent using the glue--glue has the capacity to make the paper soggy or warp your masterpiece. It is almost practically difficult to have too little glue. Do not forget to hold the pieces together for at least twenty seconds!

5 - Finished.

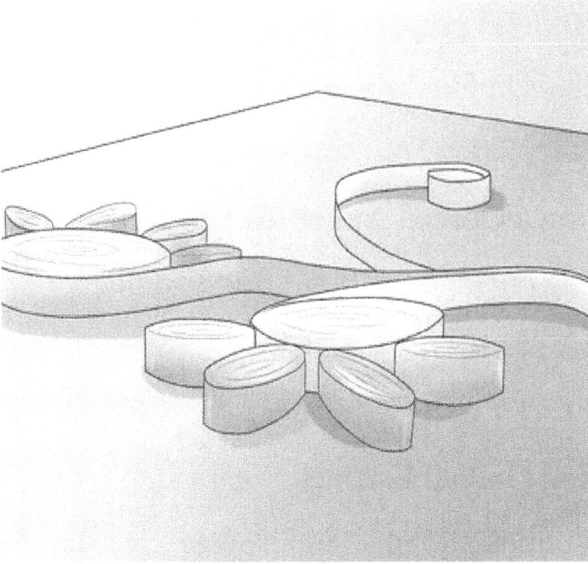

6 – Attempt some patterns and projects.

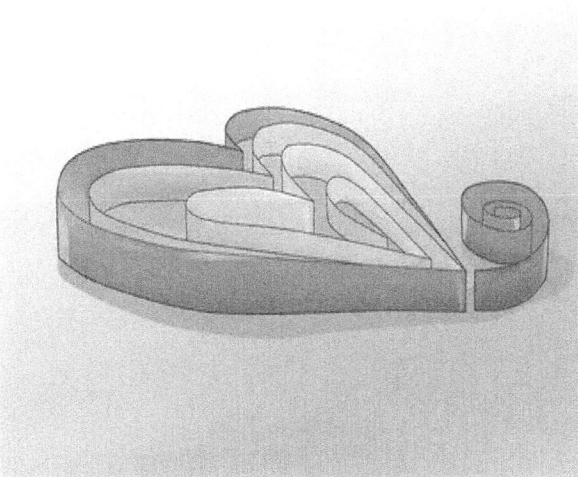

You can get to a craft store and purchase a book of quilling patterns. Try some patterns and projects included in this beginner's book! These patterns and projects include:

- **Making a Quilled Angel.** This design makes a beautiful angel that will bring about cherished gift or a cute Christmas tree topper.

- **Making Quilled Earrings.** Learn step by step instructions to make domes, cones, or flat designs and piece them together into stylish ear jewelry.

CHAPTER SEVEN

How to Make Quilling Earrings

<u>Quilling</u> is the process of coiling paper and forming the coils into various different designs. Quilling is a simple, easy and fun way to make earring designs. There are several diverse ways to create quilling earrings. You can shape the quilling into cones and domes, leave the paper quilling coiled flat to create amazing designs, or make a combination of the two types of quilling designs. After you have gotten your quilling designs, you will embellish them, glue or string them together, and afterward join them to earring hooks to create your designs into earrings.

Part 1 – Creating A Dome Or Cone Design
1 - Join strips of quilling with glue.

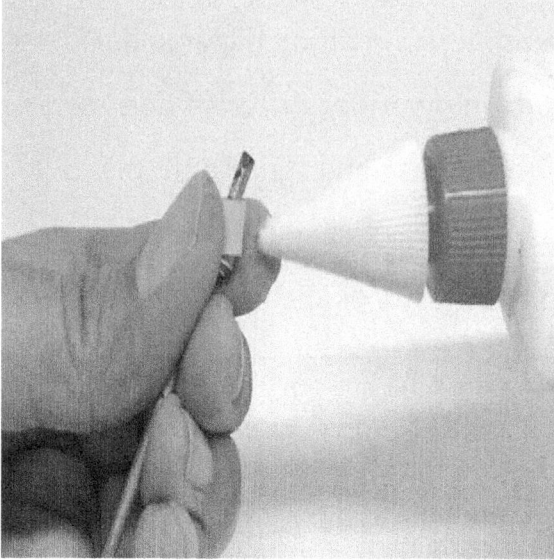

Utilize some glue to join five of the paper quilling strips together. Place a dot of glue on the end of each strip and utilize this to connect it to the following strip. You will require the extra material to create a dome or cone.

2 - Coil the paper quilling.

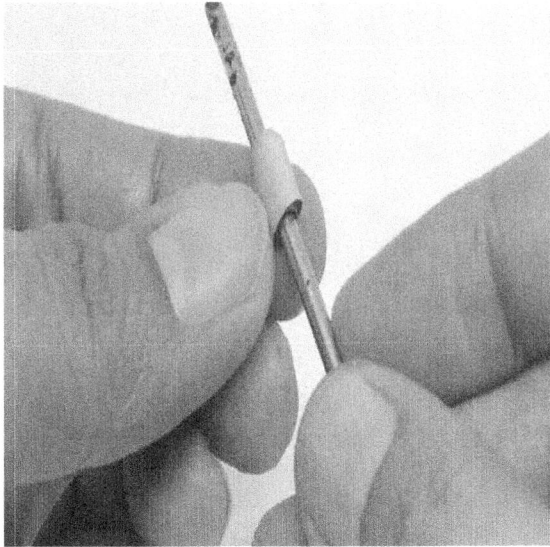

Start coiling the paper quilling utilizing a quilling needle. Wrap the quilling paper around the needle again and again until it shapes a tight coil.

- It is essential to make a tight coil when making quilling cones and domes. This will look preferred and better secure than a loose coil.

3 - Utilize a dome or cone shaped object to make the coil.

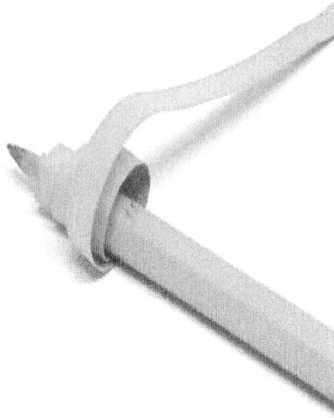

When you have made the coil, you can start to push out the middle to shape the coil into a cone or dome. Utilize a quilling small mold to shape the quilling into a dome shape. Press the coil over the small mold to shape it into a dome.

- If you don't have a small mold, then you can as well utilize a thimble to assist you shape the coil. Or, you can likewise simply utilize the tip of your fingertip, but your results may not be as exactly.

Part 2 – Making Flat Designs

1 – Select your colors.

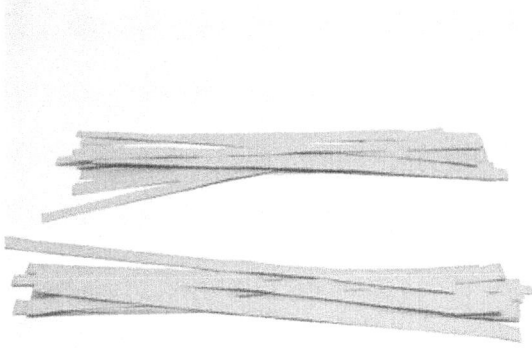

The colors you make use of can alter the result or outcome of your project. Quilling comes in wide range of colors, so you have heaps of options. Try to choose a couple of various types of quilling in coordinating colors.

- For instance, you could select black and white quilling, green and pink, or blue and yellow and blue. Choose colors that appear good to you and that will work for your design.

- Consider the way you want your design to look like also. For instance, if you are creating heart shapes, then select pinks and reds. If you are making a cone for a Christmas tree, at that point utilize green quilling.

2 - Coil the quilling.

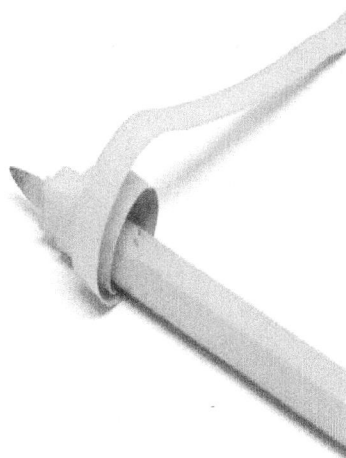

You should utilize a quilling needle to coil your quilling. Wrap the end of the quilling over the quilling needle and afterward start to turn the needle to wrap the quilling around it. Continue turning the needle and coiling the quilling until you come to the end.

- To make your coils bigger, utilize numerous strips of quilling. Simply glue the ends of the strips together prior to coiling them.
- For flat quilling designs, you should coil the quilling firmly or leave it loose to make various designs.

3 - Shape the designs.

You can shape the level coils into various shapes by pushing on the edges. You can leave the quilling around, squeeze the sides to make it into an oval, or push on every four sides to shape it into a square.

- You can make a heart formed quilling design by making two coils, loosening them slightly, and afterward squeezing them on the ends to create a teardrop design. After that, glue the 2 pieces together along the flat edges to make a heart shape.

- You could even try utilizing a mold to enable you shape your quilling. For instance, if you have a little star shaped cookie cutter, at that point you could put a loose spiral into the mold and push out towards the edges of the mold to frame the shape into a star.

Part 3- Putting Your Designs Together

1 - Paint your designs.

You can utilize puffy paint or some customary acrylic paint to add enthusiasm to your quilling earring pieces. Try to add some polka dots around the edges or paint over the whole piece with a strong color.

- If you need to include some fine details, you can paint them onto the quilling pieces, such as initials or a word or some little flowers. Utilize a fine tipped paint brush to make it simpler to make little designs on your quilling pieces.

2 - Add beads and sequins.

You can as well glue some sequins and/or beads onto your quilling piece. Try to add a border of beads to the base edge of a dome shaped quilling piece. Or, include some sequins around the top and side edges of a level or flat quilling piece to include some sparkle.

- You can try to add other notions to your quilling designs also. For instance, if you feel some little pom poms would look cute, you can glue some on. If you desire to add a button, go for it!

3 – You have to glue or string multiple pieces together.

After you have made your quilling pieces for the studs or earrings, you can either stick them together or string them together. The way that you join your pieces relies upon the types of pieces you have made.

- For instance, if you have made a wide range of various sized cones or domes, then it would likely be better to string them together utilizing a needle and some nylon thread.

- For flat pieces, it might be simpler to glue them together and allow them sit until they are dry. You can stick together various sized coils together inside of a big coil, or glue a couple of various pieces together to make a shape, such as a flower. In any case, you will even now need to add a string to join the quilling stud or earring pieces to the earring hooks.

- If you have different pieces that you need to hang from the earrings, ensure to string them

together in the manner or way you desire
them to appear.

4 - Join earring hooks or studs.

When you are pleased with your quilling earring
pieces, you can either connect them to earring
hooks or studs.

- To finish hook style quilling earrings, insert
  the top side of the string via the hoop and
  bind it to secure the quilling pieces to the
  earring hook.

- In order to finish earrings on studs, stick the
  quilling piece to the earring stud and let to
  dry for various hours or overnight.

CHAPTER EIGHT

Step By Step Guide To Create An Angel Out Of Quilling Paper

Follow the steps below to create an angel out of quilling paper.

Steps

1- Take a wide quilling strip for the angel's body.

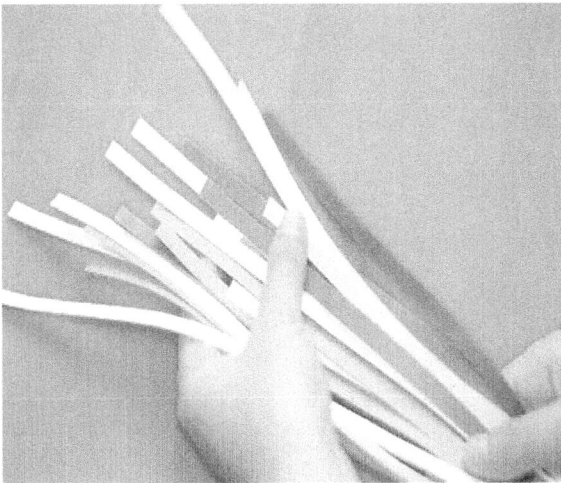

Select an angelic color, or any color you desire. Utilize white and paint your finished Angel if you prefer.

2 – You have to roll the quilling strip as well as apply glue to it to secure the end.

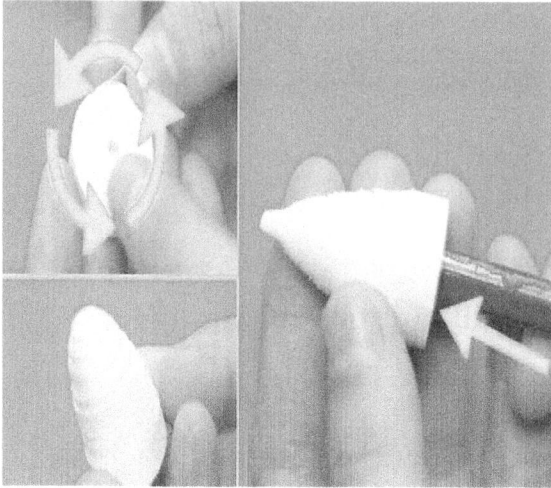

Form the circle a cone shape by means of pushing it upwards. Push tenderly; try not to make a cylinder, except you need little tubby angels - which actually could be cute.

3 - Make arms.

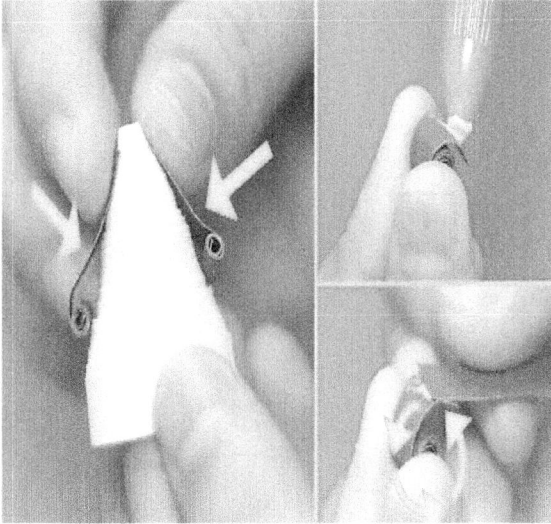

Utilize an extremely narrow strip of paper rolled at the end to form hands. Now, glue these to the body of your angel. You can make use of pipe cleaners for arms as well or simply stick paper or card cut into arm shapes onto the holy angel.

4 - Make the face.

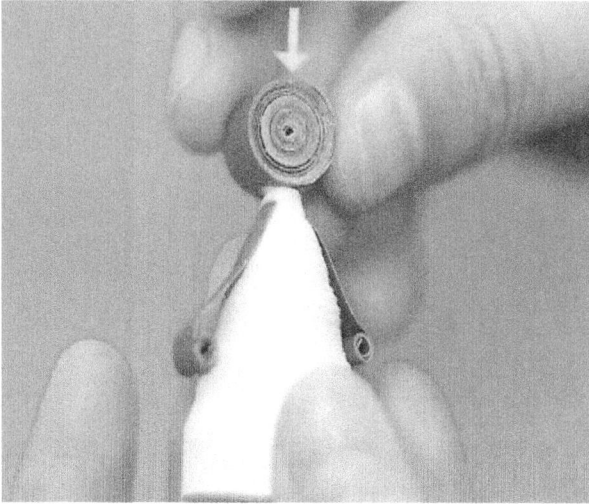

Join three thin strips together and roll it into a coil that makes a fittingly sized head. Wooden beads can likewise be utilized as heads if wanted. Glue your angels head to her or his body. Angels can be young men as well!

5 - Allow all the glue dry thoroughly.

Apply more if needed. The arms and head of your angel need to be solidly attatched.

6 – Be sure to roll small circles at the ends of quilling strips for the hair.

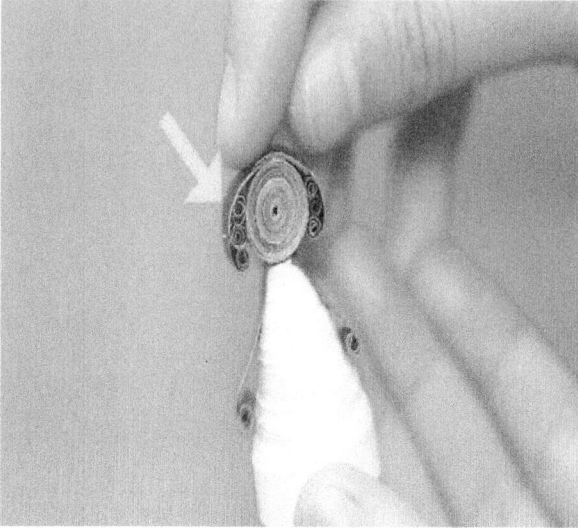

Your angel can be a redhead or brunette, blonde. You could utilize thread or wool for the hair as well.

7 - Attach all these circles so that it would appear like hair, or glue on wool.

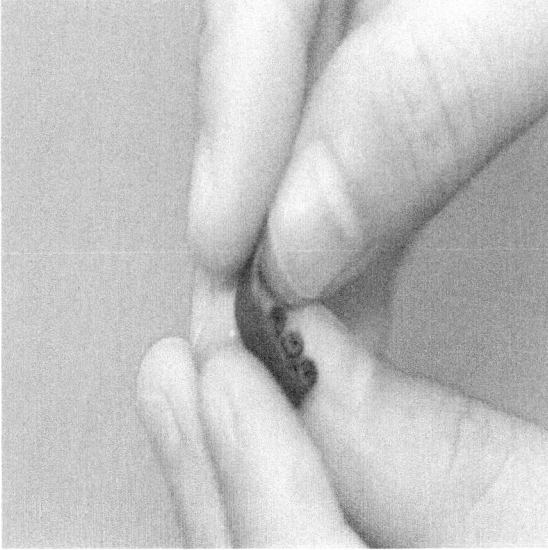

Try to make the hair tithe same on both sides. Include a halo of gold thread, paper or card. You can either stick a circle behind the angels head, or attach a strip in a circle around the head.

8 – You have to make the wings by means of rolling a strip and loosening it.

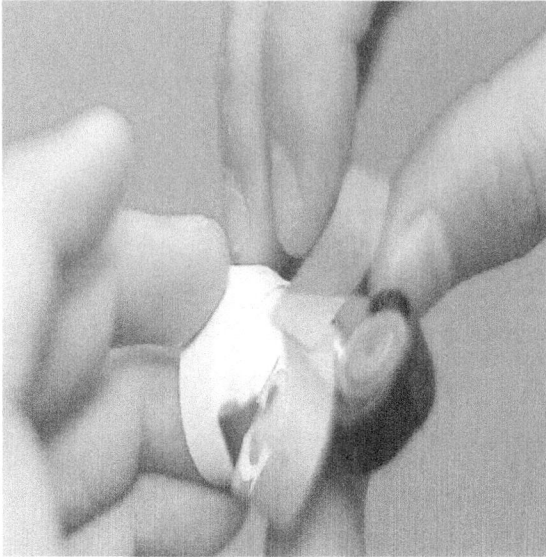

Make wings from little feathers, card or whatever thing else you consider suitable or appropriate. Ensure to glue the wings to your angels back.

9 – Include a circle of black cotton to the back of your angel's head if you desire to hang it from your Christmas tree.

If you make many, don't bother if they are not all precisely the same. Hand crafted items are expected to be unique.

CHAPTER NINE

Paper Quilled Teardrop Vase

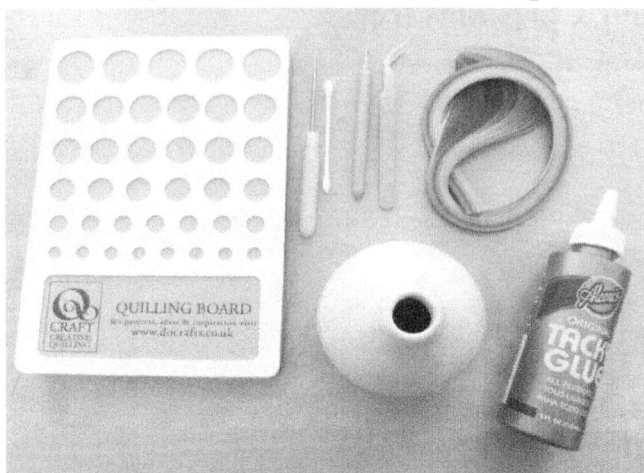

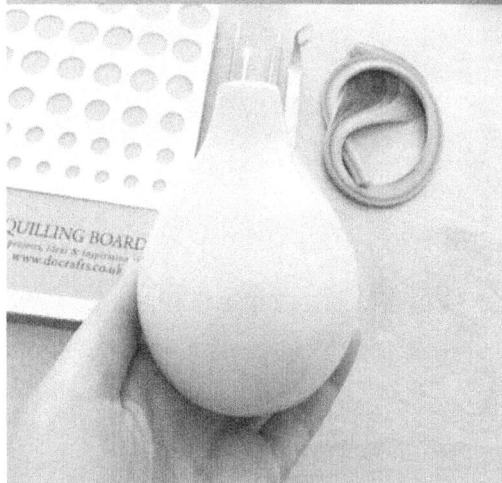

This project is not complex to do especially for beginners and the tools and materials are inexpensive.

What you will need:

- A vase: An opaque vase that has no extreme curves but only smooth and gentle curves and not too big

- Paper strips in a gradient of colours

- Glue:I made used of Aleene's tacky glue.

- Quilling slotted tool

- Quilling needle tool: You can make use of a cocktail stick as well, or anything you can use to apply glue precisely.

- Quilling board (optional):

Step 1: Roll the Paper Spirals

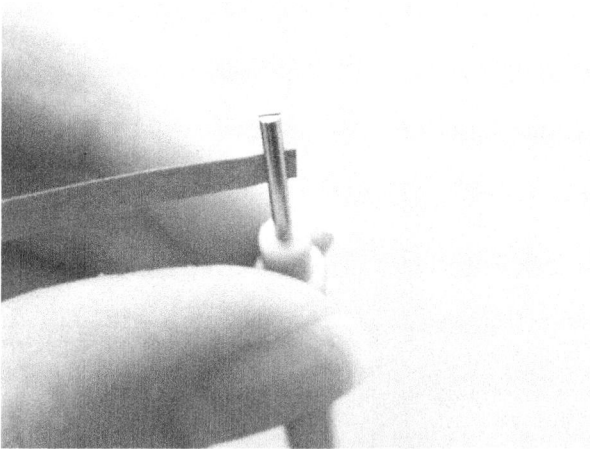

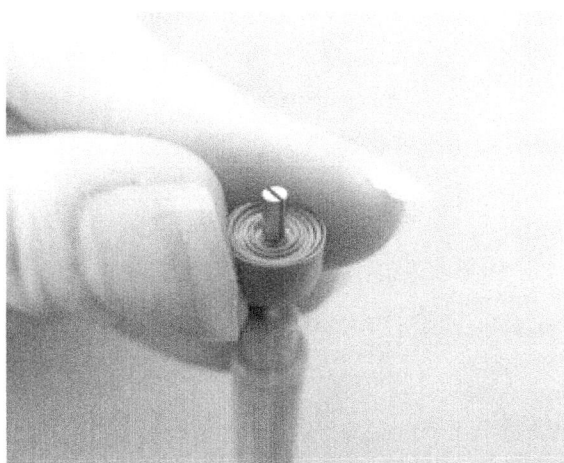

Beginning with the darkest colour of paper you are going to make use of, place the very end of one paper strip into the slotted tool.

You have to rotate the tool while holding the paper strip so that the paper wraps tightly around the metal rod.

It's not very important, but the paper strips have one smoother side and one rougher side, so endeavor and keep the smoother side on the outside of the spiral.

As you rotate the tool, keep the forming spiral resting on a finger to control it and keep it from becoming loose or getting into a mess.

Once you have made the all strip into a coil, place the coil into a circle on the quilling board and allow it slowly unfurl to fill the hole shaped guide. I utilized the third hole down which is 17mm across.

If you cannot get a quillling board, you can utilize a drawn circle guide or a ruler and cautiously allow the coil become looser until it reaches the size you desire.

Then you have to put a tiny bit of glue at the end of the paper strip, on the inside, to hold the coil in that shape. You can utilize a quilling needle or cocktail stick to apply the glue precisely.

Step 2: Form the Teardrops

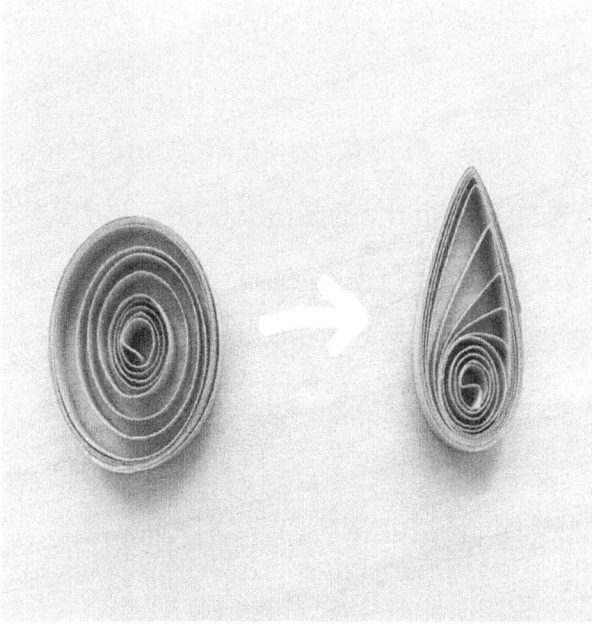

You have to take each of the coils you make and afterward turn them into teardrop shapes.

This is actually easy and all you have to do is lightly squash half of the coil between your finger and thumb, and pinch one end to craft a sharp fold.

It's up to your what sizes you make your teardrops and relies mostly upon the size of your vase. I made four rows of one size and afterward made teardrops of a smaller size for the top row.

Step 3: Add the Teardrops to the Vase

Step 4: Finished!

CHAPTER TEN

Step By Step Guide To Make A Paper Quilled Photo Frame

A cute and in-a-budget gift idea for your loved ones. Create a quilled paper flower photo frame!

What You Need

1. Foam board

2. X-acto knife and scissor

3. Strong adhesive glue and craft glue

4. Pencil and ruler

5. Quilling paper

6 Beads.

Instructions

Step-1:

Firstly, make sure to measure your photo size and cut out two pieces of foam board adding extra 2 inches on both width and length of the photo size. Draw 1 inch frame around any one piece and an upside down arch shape directly in the top center part of the other piece. See the picture. Cut out the frame (the piece with borders) as neatly as possible. Ensure to cut out the arch shape neatly as well

Step-2:

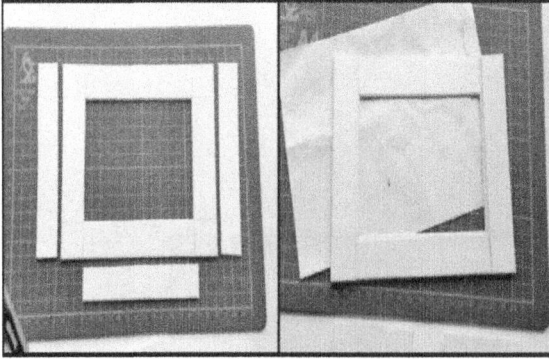

Right now place the frame on a plain surface. Measure and cut 3 pieces from the froth board for the sides and base part of the foam. Glue the pieces perfectly along their place. The top side of the frame ought to remain open. This is for inserting the photo into the frame.

Step-3:

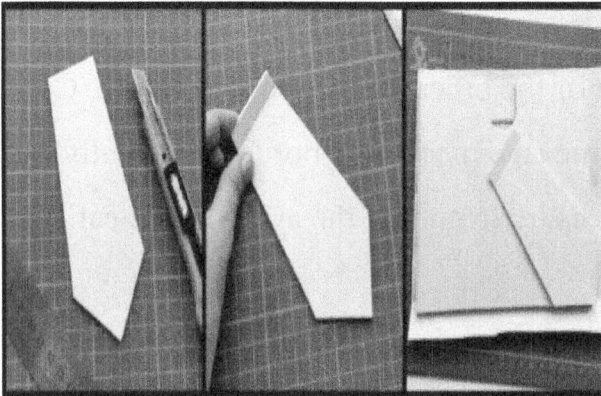

Ensure to cut out a tie shaped pattern from the foam board for the stand. Form a half cut along the top 1 .5 cm of the stand and twist it. Glue the back part of the frame and afterward glue the 1.5 cm part of the stand on the back side diagonally by keeping the corner coordinated with the corner of the frame.

Step-4:

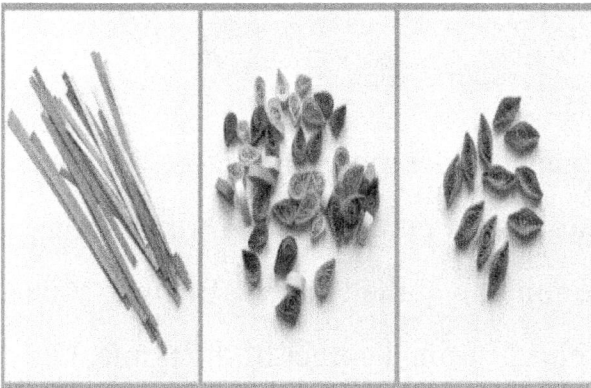

Get ready papers strips for qulling. Make use of bright colors for the flowers and green for the leaves. Utilize the bright colored paper strips to create teardrop shaped pattern. Make as many as you require to make flowers. Utilize the green colored paper strips to make leaf shaped pattern. Make as many as you need.

Step-5:

Put a scrap paper under the frame before beginning the paper quilling art on the frame. Utilize white / craft glue to join the quilled papers. Begin to glue the quilled papers from a corner of the frame. Only glue and position them. I utilized six teardrop pattern for each flower. You might add more petals if you feel like. Glue additional patterns to make a chain of flowers.

Step-6:

Make more paper quilling flowers all around the
frame. Strive to keep a pleasant color
combination. Glue the leaves amid the flowers. I
also included some faux pearl beads on the middle
of the flowers and some loose quilled circles in the
little gaps.

CHAPTER ELEVEN

How To Make A Paper Quilled Monogram

History of the Paper Quilled Monogram

Quilling is a papercraft that has been around for hundreds of years and is still popular today. Rolling paper strips into beautiful works of art is easy enough even for beginners to achieve impressive results. You don't have to spend a lot of money to get started with this craft either. All you require is just paper, glue and a round object such as a toothpick or a bamboo skewer to curl the paper strips.

Several crafters make quilled monograms to offer as wedding gifts, or to make use of as wall decor.

Supplies Needed:

- Cardstock or precut quilling strips in desired colors
- A thick sheet of cardstock or board to use as the background
- A sheet of Cardstock for background
- Scissors
- Craft paper trimmer
- Mod Podge or tacky glue
- small-sized paintbrush
- Paper Plate or old plastic container
- Tweezers
- Shadowbox Picture Frame

Print Your Outline

1. Print your letter of preference in a light gray color onto the cardstock background.

2. An alternative means is to print the letter filled with black onto a sheet of paper, and afterward place the black letter print behind the piece of paper you plan to utilize as the monogram background. Place both sheets next to a window and trace the letter with a pencil by hand onto the cardstock background. You have to make straight

lines with a ruler and pencil tracing over the transfer pencil marks.

3. Wipe away any dark or stray pencil marks.

Cut the Paper Strips

1. Choose cardstock in colors you plan to incorporate into your design.

2. Cut one-quarter inch wide paper strips with a paper cutter from the colored cardstock.

3. You can purchase precut quilling strips online or at the craft store if you desire to skip this step. The option is yours.

Shape the Paper Strips

Six Common Types of Rolled Quilling Shapes

Tight Circle

Loose Circle

V Scroll

Open Heart

(loose scroll image)

Loose Scroll

C Scroll

1. Choose what the design of the inside of your letter would be. It helps to look at photos for inspiration and make a preliminary swift thumbnail sketch for the layout of your monogram.

2. Make your shapes utilizing a toothpick or quilling tool. Obtain your paper strip and wind it around your toothpick into the shape preferred. Place a little glue onto the end of the paper strip to keep the shape in place. If you desire a tighter more compact paper shape, roll it tightly. If you need a looser paper shape, roll it loosely.

3. It is an excellent idea to practice making diverse shapes until you get the hang of it. It requires some effort and patience to master the art of paper quilling, but if you are unrelenting, you will soon be making lovely works of art.

Glue the Quilled Paper Strips

There is one significant concept to remember while gluing your quilling strips: "Less is more" is the first rule when it comes to gluing quilling strips to your baseboard. You can ruin your project with too much glue, so be careful. Some people utilize a small brush to apply glue to the bottom of the quilling strips and afterward place and hold the strips onto the background until the paper pieces can stand up on their own.

Other people find that placing the quilling strips onto a paper plate with glue and afterward placing on the background works better for them. You need to practice and choose which method works for you.

Just remember to make use of a light touch while applying the glue to your paper strips.

Frame the Outside of the Letter With Paper Strips

The most vital step of the quilled monogram procedure is to build a paper frame around your letter. Glue and set your strips, holding them until the glue is firm enough for the strip to stand up on its own. Ensure to have a one-quarter inch overlap on the ends of the paper strips, and secure the strips by a drop of glue. Allow the "wall" of your quilled monogram to dry very well before proceeding to the next step.

Start Filling in Your Letter Frame

Once you have built your outside frame, it is time to fill in the insides of your monogram. You have to follow the design in your draft and glue your shapes and strips into place. Allow the finished piece to dry fully for a few hours.

Tweezers Are a Quillers Best Friend

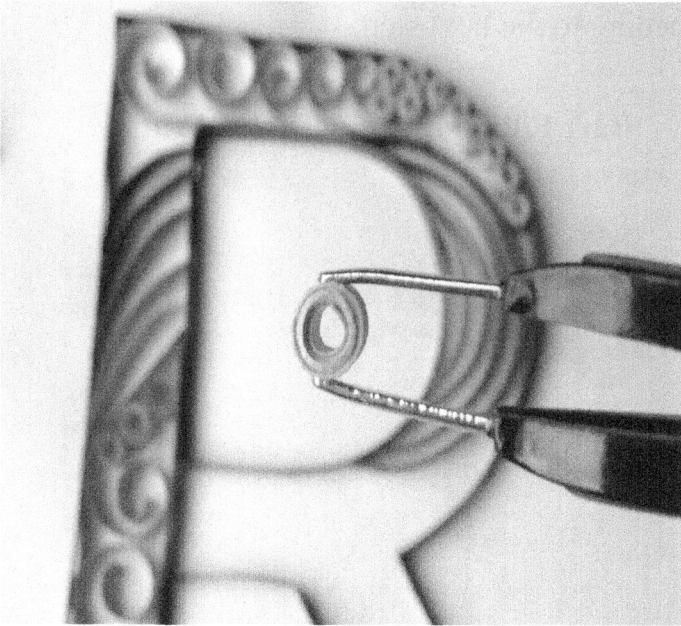

Tweezers are one of the most significant tools you will use. Tweezers will go where your fingers cannot, saving you time and alleviating frustration.

Frame the Finished Quilled Monogram

Once you have finished your project, you will want to put your quilled monogram into a frame. If you make use of a usual picture frame you will have to take away the protective glass from the front. There simply isn't sufficient room to allow for the raised surface of the quilled paper in a standard frame. If having the piece protected by the glass is significant to you, you will discover that a shadowbox frame would solve your problems. Shadowbox frames have an inch or more depth under the protective glass and are just right to frame your quilled art piece.

Made in the USA
Monee, IL
30 November 2020